Introduction

Scotland's coastline is an astonishing 11,800km long! That's twice the length of the English coast and longer than the entire eastern coastline of the United States of America; 8% of all the coastline in Europe is Scottish!

The range of landforms and habitats which make up the Scottish coastline is outstanding; from towering cliffs in Orkney and St Kilda to the broad machair plains of the Uists, and the shifting dunes of Sutherland and Aberdeenshire. In the west, sheltered sea lochs provide a stark contrast to the exposed rocky shores of the open coast. In the east the predominantly low-lying coastline, dominated by dune-fringed sandy beaches, is cut into by the Firths of Moray, the Tay and the Forth as well as numerous smaller inlets. Add to this nearly 800 vegetated islands and it's easy to see why Scotland's coast is so long and so diverse.

There is no one point in Scotland more than 65km from the coast, and a significant proportion of the population lives within only a few kilometres of it. Throughout history the sea has had an important influence on Scotland's development and the people that live and visit there; this influence continues today. Many livelihoods still depend directly or indirectly upon the sea: important resources, such as food, oil and gas, are harvested there; we are still dependent on the sea for the transportation of people and materials, and the coast remains many peoples' favoured holiday destination.

Having fun on the beach at Camas á Mhór-bheòil, Skye

Evolution of the coastline

The Ice Age

Scotland's coastline has not always appeared as it does today. If it were possible to travel back in time 20,000 years, you would see a very different landscape. Back then, the planet was still in the grips of the last Ice Age and sea levels were around 140m lower than they are today. As a result, the English Channel and most of what is now the North Sea was dry land, making it possible for animals to travel between Britain and continental Europe. The edge of the Atlantic Ocean lay many kilometres west of the Hebrides.

In addition, a vast ice sheet up to 1.5km thick - around the same height as Ben Nevis - blanketed Scotland. The coast resembled that of the Arctic today, with pack-ice in winter and icebergs breaking off from the glaciers into the ocean waters.

Rising seas

The extent of the ice sheet covering Britain 20,000 years ago

Scotland's coastline only began to take on its present appearance following the melting of the last ice sheet between 15,000 and 10,000 years ago. As the glaciers retreated they left behind a barren landscape, carved out by the scouring actions of the massive ice sheets and glacial meltwater. The melting ice resulted in sea levels rising dramatically, by up to 15mm per year. The Atlantic engulfed the low-lying continental shelf around Britain, finally separating England from France about 8,000 years ago. In Scotland the seas flooded the ice-scoured landscape. Groups of islands, such as Orkney and Shetland, were created and the lower lying river channels and glacial valleys were submerged to form many of the firths evident today, such as those of the Clyde and Tay.

Sea loch formed by flooding of ancient valley due to rising seas, Whiteness Voe, Shetland

Ancient cliffline and beach now raised clear of the sea by rising land, west coast of Arran

Ancient peat beds now submerged at high tide by rising seas, The Houb, Shetland

The land bounces back

Even today, sea levels around the world continue to rise, though at only around 2mm per year. In spite of this, much of the Scottish coastline has actually been rising slowly back out of the sea again for the last 6,000 years. This is due to the Scottish landmass bouncing back upwards following its release from the crushing weight of ice which formerly lay upon it. Uplift has been greatest where the ice was thickest, around the Western Highlands, and least in areas closer to the margins of the ancient ice sheet, such as the Western Isles, Orkney and Shetland.

The lifting of the land in Scotland, together with rising sea levels worldwide, has produced a range of distinctive coastal features. In areas where land uplift has been more rapid than sea-level rise, ancient cliffs and beaches have gradually been lifted beyond the reach of the waves and are today stranded up to 40m above high-water mark. Striking examples of these raised beaches and sea cliffs occur around Arran, Jura, Islay and the Inner Hebrides.

In contrast, where sea-level rise has outpaced uplift of the land, as in Orkney, Shetland and the Western Isles, drowning of the landscape still continues. This is clearly shown by the presence of peat beds, complete with tree roots, once formed on land but now covered by the sea.

Beach formation

During and immediately after the Ice Age, the glaciers and rivers carried millions of tonnes of sand and gravel towards the sea. Many of these deposits still remain submerged but others have been re-worked by the power of the waves, mixed with shell debris and driven onto the land to make the sand and shingle beaches we see today.

Sand ripples, Lingay Strand, Newton, North Uist

Waves breaking on shingle

The changing coast

By around 5,000 years ago Scotland's coastline looked similar to todays but, even so, things still continue to change.

Sea-level rise continues to affect the Northern and Western Isles, slowly flooding low-lying areas. Elsewhere, beaches and other non-rocky coastlines are being eroded, such as at Montrose in Angus where some sand dunes are retreating up to 4m each year. The exact opposite is occurring in other places. At Tentsmuir in Fife, some of the anti-tank defences built on the shore during the Second World War now lie over 100m inland.

Even on Scotland's rockiest coastlines, changes are occurring. The Old Man of Hoy in Orkney, appears to symbolise permanence, yet this world famous structure was only created around 150 years ago when a rock arch linking it to the cliffs of Hoy collapsed during a storm.

The wind

The wind can have a dramatic affect on our coast, especially in dune systems. Sand dunes first started building up around the Scottish coast about 5,000 years ago. From time to time they became unstable and the wind flattened them, blowing the sand inland. At Eoligarry on Barra, coastal sand smothers the hillside 100m above sea level! This process continues today, creating great waves of bare sand which drift across the landscape.

Long-shore drift

Large volumes of sand and shingle are also being driven along and around the coast, partly by the tide but primarily by the force of the waves. This process is known as long-shore drift and it occurs wherever waves strike a beach at an angle. It is dramatically shown by shingle spits which may grow by anything from 5 to 100m each year such as at Speymouth.

Seasonal change

Even over the course of a year most beaches can change dramatically in appearance. In prolonged calm weather sand tends to collect at the top of the shore but when winter storms strike, it is often scoured away by the waves and dumped on the sea bed around or below low-water mark. This seemingly annual cycle can result in beaches rising and falling by a metre or more each year.

Old Man of Hoy, Orkney

North Uist looking towards South Harris

Sand dunes, Sands of Forvie

Shingle spits, Speymouth

Historical changes

The coastline of Scotland has not only been shaped by natural forces but, over the last few centuries especially, it has also been strongly influenced by people. From the time Scotland was first inhabited, 9,000 years ago, people have settled on the coast; they were attracted by the fertile ground, the rich food resources of the sea, and the advantages for transport and opportunities for trade that the sea provides. Early communities adopted a subsistence way of life which, in comparison to today, had a low impact on the natural heritage of the coast; these communities lived in relative harmony with their environment.

However, major social and economic changes over the last few hundred years in Scotland have resulted in dramatic changes to the character and natural heritage of the coastline. More intensive farming, coastal development and increased access to the coast have all hindered the natural coastal processes and led to a loss of habitat and wild coastal land. The cities of Glasgow, Edinburgh, Dundee and Aberdeen have grown and spread along the coastline and numerous towns have developed, mostly as fishing ports, on mainland and island coasts alike. Outside these settlements, the density of people is still relatively low. However, despite over 85% of the coast being undeveloped, there are few stretches of coast where signs of habitation are completely absent.

Neolithic house, Bosta, Great Bernera

Distribution of coastal habitats

- Sand dunes and machair
- Sea cliffs
- Saltmarsh
- Shingle

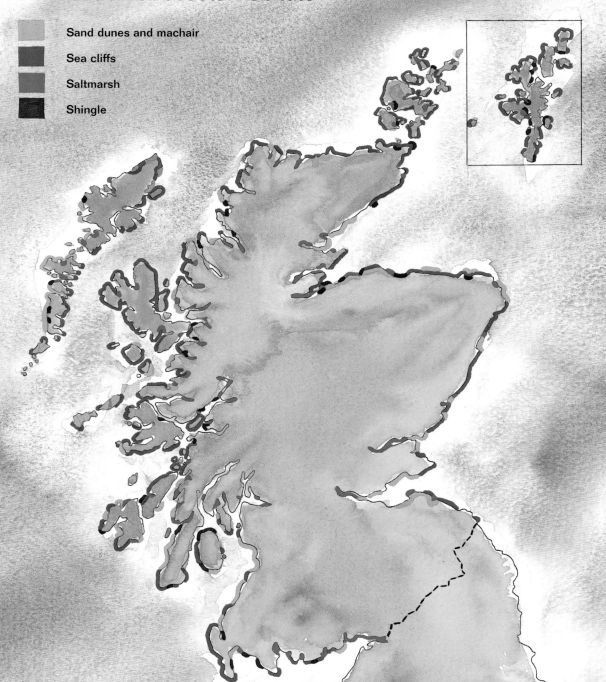

9

Life on the coast

The coastal zone is a fascinating place - it forms the interface between the sea and the land. These two environments are so different, however, that there is very little overlap and the high-water mark forms a distinct boundary between marine and terrestrial life.

Above this boundary sand dunes and machair, saltmarsh, shingle and cliffs provide habitats for a wealth of wildlife highly adapted to suit the conditions that, although essentially terrestrial, are still strongly influenced by the sea. Plants and animals have to cope with the specific stresses that living by the sea brings, such as drought, exposure, highly mobile mud and sand, salt spray and even occasional flooding by salty sea water. In this hostile environment, wildlife often require clever adaptations to survive. Only very few flowering plants, such as eel grass which grows along with seaweeds in the intertidal zone, are able to survive below the high-water mark.

Only a limited number of plants are even able to live near the high-water mark. Those, such as glasswort and sea blite, which make up the lower saltmarsh and do get regularly flooded by the tide, have succulent leaves which prevent the plant drying out when uncovered by water. Sea rocket forms an annual strandline vegetation and marram grass actually grows better if buried by sand and, therefore, thrives in sand dunes. Sea thrift is able to cling onto rocky shores and cliffs despite there being minimal soil cover. Moving further inland, away from the stressful impacts of the sea, particularly salt spray, other less tolerant plants become more common and the floral richness increases.

Of all the animals, birds are the most obvious and vocal inhabitants of the coastline. In spring and summer months, sea cliffs come alive with seabirds squabbling and bickering over nesting sites. In comparison, over the winter months sheltered estuaries teem with hundreds of thousands of waders and wildfowl attracted by the plentiful food and safe roosts of the mudflats and saltmarsh. Just as important are the mammals, amphibians and invertebrates which characterise the different coastal habitats and have adapted to life by the sea.

Eel grass

Knot

Natterjack toad

Sea rocket

Habitats

Sand dunes

Sandy beaches occur all around the coast but are especially common in Aberdeenshire, Orkney and the Inner and Outer Hebrides, where they can appear to stretch endlessly into the distance. Wherever there are strong onshore winds and a low-lying coastal plain where sand can accumulate, dunes may develop.

Initially, dunes begin to form where wind-blown sand collects around the debris cast from the sea at the top of the beach. Dune-building grasses soon appear; in particular the tall tussocky marram grass, which characterises dunes in this country. These grasses themselves act as a buffer to the wind, trapping more sand, so that the dune grows in height and width. Exceptionally, as at Balnakiel in Sutherland and Crossapol on Coll, dunes may reach 35m or more in height! The grasses also stabilise the sand surface, making it more hospitable for other plants and animals to colonise.

Moving inland the mobile dunes change to more stable 'fixed' dunes as the amount of blown sand reduces. As conditions become easier in which to live, many other grasses and herbs become established to form a grassland or heathland.

Blowout in dune ridge

Dune-binding grasses colonising embryonic dunes

Heathland developing on acidic sands inland

Machair

In the north-west of Scotland, the strength of the winds produces a distinctive coastal landscape which is found hardly anywhere else in the world. On many exposed coastlines, the extreme winds blow sand inland which smothers the land and forms a broad, flat plain between the beaches and the hills. The name given by the Gaelic speaking people of such areas to this unique and important landform is 'mhachair' (or 'machair' as it is known in English), and it characterises most of the length of the Western Isles, as well as other islands on the north-west coast.

Machair sand is largely made up of tiny shell fragments. Being calcareous (calcium-rich), these provide an ideal soil which encourages a very rich grassland to develop; in summer months the flowering plants form a dazzling mosaic of colour stretching into the distance. Closely linked with the machair grassland are salty lagoons, freshwater lochs and fens, providing a wealth of different habitats for plants, birds and other animals.

Traditional agricultural use of machair

Fresh deposits of blown sand carpet the machair grassland following storms

Machair flowers

15

Saltmarsh

Saltmarsh is a relatively rare habitat in Scotland. It is found in river estuaries, deeply indented sea lochs and behind sand or shingle bars, where there is little or no exposure to wave action. In Scotland, the most extensive saltmarsh areas occur in the sheltered upstream areas of the Tay, Forth and Solway Firths and within bays and sea lochs on the west coast. In such places, fine sediment settles out onto the shore and forms mudflats, sometimes many hundreds of metres wide. Certain flowering plants such as glasswort, a succulent plant often harvested for food on the Continent, and saltmarsh grass, may then establish in the mud at the top of the shore.

Moving inland, away from the sea, the saltmarsh is flooded less often and so other plants, less tolerant of sea water, become established. Sea thrift, for instance, can be so common that, in early summer, the saltmarsh turns into a vast pink carpet of flowers. This process of succession continues inland until the influence of the sea disappears and there is a change to terrestrial or freshwater habitats.

In winter, estuaries are extremely important roosting and feeding sites for hundreds of thousands of over-wintering waders and wildfowl such as dunlin, widgeon and brent geese. These birds travel from as far away as the Arctic to feed on the mud flats, saltmarsh and surrounding areas. In summer, they are replaced by breeding birds such as redshank and ringed plover.

Glasswort growing in sand to form lower saltmarsh

Saltmarsh with sea thrift in flower

Dunlin

17

Sea cliffs

High, rocky cliffs dominate the Scottish coastline, providing some of Britain's most spectacular coastal scenery. The highest cliffs in Britain, soaring to 430m, are found on the remote islands of St Kilda where they withstand the full force of the Atlantic Ocean.

In summer months the cliffs belong to the seabirds. Tens of thousands of guillemots, kittiwakes, fulmars, razorbills and many more crowd onto the steep cliffs to lay their eggs and rear their young. Others, such as puffins and manx shearwaters choose to burrow into the steep slopes to nest.

Due to their inaccessibility, to all but the seabirds, cliffs are one of the least modified habitats in Scotland. The hard, near vertical rock faces, broken only by a few ledges and cracks and battered by the wind and waves do not, at first sight, appear a very hospitable environment for life. However, even here, lichens and salt-tolerant plants, such as sea thrift and Scot's lovage, are able to set root wherever a thin soil can build up in crevices and on ledges. Higher up the cliffs and on the cliff tops, out of reach of the waves but still influenced by saltspray, a richer maritime grassland or heathland develops.

Dore Holm, near Esha Ness, Shetland

Thrift-clad cliff, Handa Island

Kittiwakes and shags

Shingle

Shingle beaches occur all around Scotland but particularly in the Moray Firth, the Hebrides and the Northern Isles. Most of the stones which make up such beaches were formed by erosion of the land during the Ice Age, and were carried to the coast by the glaciers and rivers. Since then they have been reworked and rounded by the constant action of the waves.

Shingle beaches are widespread but 'stabilised' shingle with vegetation is relatively rare because few plants are able to colonise this mobile and often exposed substrate. Those that do are typically annual species, such as orache, which die back every year during the winter storms. A more complete plant cover is only able to develop further inland, where the surface has become more stable and a soil layer has developed.

The top of shingle beaches above the spring tide level, especially on exposed coastlines, is often marked by a distinctive ridge of pebbles, known as a storm beach. In places, whole series or 'staircases' of these storm beaches have been formed and stranded inland as the high-water mark has retreated seaward. Elsewhere, shingle may accumulate as distinctive spits, extending hundreds of metres along the coast, or as bars linking separate islands.

Shingle storm beach with ancient raised beach in background, Rum

Common orache

Hooked shingle spits, Culbin

Human Influences

Recreation

In spite of the notoriously unpredictable Scottish weather, the coast is still a hugely popular place to go for holidays or a day out. Residents and visitors alike are attracted by the sandy beaches, striking scenery and the chance to 'get away from it all'. It provides limitless scope to watch wildlife, pursue outdoor sports such as diving and sailing, or simply walk, contemplate and seek inspiration.

For everyone's benefit it is essential to maintain those qualities that make the coast so special - its beauty, diversity and wildness. Visitor pressure alone can severely damage the natural environment of the coast. Too much trampling encourages dune erosion. Beaches may be spoilt by litter and sewage. Poorly sited caravan parks can become an eyesore on otherwise wild beaches. The coastline is a fragile environment and we need to be aware of how much impact our own activities may cause. This is vital if we are to conserve the quality of our coastline and ensure that it can be enjoyed by many generations to come.

Birdwatching on Shetland, Noss National Nature Reserve

Claimed arable land and forestry on the Eden Estuary

Agriculture

Ever since Scotland's people first settled along the coast, the land has been used for grazing livestock and gathering or cultivating food. More recently, however, intensive farming practices have resulted in significant changes to the environment. Natural habitats such as saltmarsh have been 'claimed' and converted to arable land so it can be farmed. Coastal vegetation has suffered from over-grazing resulting in a reduction in the range of habitats and species. An increase in the use of artificial pesticides and herbicides has altered the natural balance of plants and animals. In order to reduce these impacts farmers, crofters and landowners are now being encouraged to use environmentally sensitive farming practices.

Forestry

Within this century large areas of the coast have been planted with non-native trees. This was partly in response to the demand for timber but also in an attempt to stabilise shifting coastlines such as sand dunes. It is now better understood that the interest and value of such coastal systems depends on having present the full range of natural features and processes; this includes both erosion and build-up of sediment. Opportunities are now being identified to remove these trees from certain dune systems and to restore the dunes to their natural state.

23

Sand extraction

In the more remote parts of Scotland especially, it is not uncommon for sand or shingle to be taken from beaches or dunes. This may be used for anything from building to the filling of bunkers on golf courses or, where beach sands are particularly shelly and lime rich, for use on farmland.

Where this is done by local landowners or crofters for their own use, there is usually little impact; however, where sand and shingle is removed commercially, this can have a dramatic impact upon the appearance and natural heritage of the coastline.

The removal of sand or gravel can also have a major impact on the stability of the coastline. Little fresh sediment is being fed to the coastline today from natural sources. So, when sand or shingle is taken from a beach, it is not replaced from off-shore. Instead, the pit created is simply filled in from the surrounding beach. As a result beach levels fall, increasing erosion of the dunes or land behind. If sand or gravel must be taken then it is best taken from an area inland, where the effects can be controlled and monitored.

The effect of commercial sand extraction

Development

Less than 15% of the Scottish coastline has been developed. The rest, mainly in the Highlands and Islands, remains relatively wild and unspoilt. The most heavily developed coasts are those around the Firths of Clyde, Forth and Tay. Apart from housing and industry, these coastlines support ports and harbours, power stations, roads and railways, defence establishments and, of course, scores of golf courses and other recreational and tourist facilities.

In these areas, particularly, there is constant pressure for further development, whether linked with industry, housing or leisure. If uncontrolled, such development can gradually eat away at the character and natural heritage of the coast. Planning policies need to be sensitive to the potential damage which can be caused to natural habitats and landscapes by inappropriate or piecemeal development along the coast. If a coastal location is not essential then a new development should be directed away from the shoreline; however, if a coastal location is essential, it should be accommodated within already developed coastal areas.

Coastal development on the Firth of Clyde

Coastal defence

Much of the Scottish coastline is rocky and resists erosion. In certain areas these rocks are covered by soft material such as sand, mud or shingle. Such land is considerably less resistant to the power of the waves. Dune systems particularly can be cut back by up to 10m in one year!

Where shifting coastlines are built upon, there is usually pressure to protect the land from erosion. Yet coastal defences can create problems of their own, such as obscuring natural habitats on the shoreline. By interfering with the supply or movement of beach sediment, some defences can even increase erosion on unprotected shores nearby.

Defences are also expensive and need regular maintenance to remain effective. For these reasons, new development on such coastlines is generally inappropriate unless the location is essential to the scheme's viability. Where new defences are considered vital to protect existing development, there is a clear need to consider the wider environmental effects, particularly upon coastal evolution. Greater knowledge about how sediment moves around our coastline will help us predict where such impacts might occur and create coastal defence proposals to suit each location.

In the long run, it may prove even cheaper and less environmentally damaging to move further inland those existing buildings or facilities threatened by coastal erosion. With current forecasts of rising sea levels and possible increased storminess due to global warming this is an option that may become increasingly likely in the future.

Conservation

Over 400 Sites of Special Scientific Interest have been designated around the Scottish coast. These cover a significant proportion of the coastline and help safeguard the country's most precious coastal habitats, wildlife, landforms and rocks. More recently, around 40 of these have also been identified as Special Areas of Conservation or Special Protection Areas. This means they are of European importance for the habitats, animals or plants that occur there. In addition, long stretches of the coast are incorporated within National Scenic Areas because of their high landscape value. Numerous other reserves and parks exist which are managed by Local Authorities and voluntary bodies such as the Scottish Wildlife Trust and the Royal Society for the Protection of Birds.

Stac Lee, St Kilda

This wide range of important coastal areas reflects the exceptionally high conservation value of Scotland's coastline. The vast majority of the coast remains undeveloped and unspoilt. The range of habitats, landforms and rocks which exist there is unique for such a small country.

Most coastal habitats and landforms have evolved over thousands of years to reach their present state. Yet, by inappropriate development, exploitation or over-use we can destroy in a few short years what has taken nature many millennia to create. This need not be so. We have a duty to safeguard for future generations our coastal natural heritage. Protected areas, such as those above, help to achieve this aim.

Scottish primrose

27

Our heritage

Scotland's coastline means a great many things to many people. It is a place to live and a place to visit; a place to work and a place to relax. Even so, most of the coastline remains wild and undeveloped; it's shape and form constantly changing, governed by the natural forces of the sea and the wind. Spectacular landscapes, teeming with wildlife, provide us with some of the most varied and stunning scenery in the world.

We can all take responsibility for looking after this unique environment. Recognition of its cultural, economic and natural heritage values as well as its vulnerabilities, should inspire us all to work together. In this way we can ensure that future generations are able to enjoy a coastal environment as exceptional as the one we have ourselves inherited.